91 Day Quest

for a Booming Business

L. Shay Rockhold

Copyright © 2013 L. Shay Rockhold

All rights reserved.

DEDICATION

To Bill -

The best mentor, cheerleader, sounding board, and friend I could have ever hoped for.

You are the bright spot in my galaxy.

W.A.N.

CONTENTS

The Beginning – Sort Of..................................vii

1. Changing Your Way of Thinking......................12
2. Why You Should Have Additional Pay Streams...19
3. Income Streams Options..............................35
4. Overwhelmed? 67
5. The Savvy Six..69
6. How to Approach Product Creation..................71
7. Examples..89
8. Conclusion..99
9. Resources..101
10. Tell Me About Your Quest..........................103
11. About the Author.....................................104

L. Shay Rockhold

THE BEGINNING – SORT OF

Years ago, I was at a gas station. Getting gas. (Shocker, I know. Stay with me.)

At the pump behind me was a car with a huge sticker on it for a work-at-home cosmetics company. There was a lady driving it, and she stepped out.

I had a work-at-home moms group at the time, so I walked over to introduce myself and invite her to the group. (I'd seen car seats in her vehicle, and I was guessing they weren't just ornaments.)

I'll never forget what happened next.

Her eyes grew wide as I came closer, and before I could even say a word, she blurted out, "You're Shay!"

I was surprised, to say the least, and told her she was right. But....how did she know who I was?

Her reply: "You're all over the Internet!"

= = = =

Now, that was back in 2005, but I remember it like it was yesterday.

And I've never forgotten that lesson.

See, I wasn't all over the Internet. I was all over the

Internet *in our local area*, for *what she was looking for*.

When she was searching online for a business group to join, she saw me in 8 of the top 10 spots. Each time she searched. For *numerous* search terms.

My picture was in the majority of those listings, so guess what? She "knew" me.

I get that today. I walk into meetings or say my name (It's a bit unusual, to be sure, so it's memorable), and I constantly get, "Hey, I know you! You lead the Carolina Business Outreach Network!" Or "Your name is so familiar! Oh yes, I heard someone mention you the other day." Or something else.

It's a good thing.

= = = =

You're going to create income streams and design a balanced, booming business.

Those pay streams will not only make money for you, but spread the word about your business.

Over time, you'll be having people "know" you, too.

It's a great feeling.

INTRODUCTION

What is the purpose of your 91 Day Quest?

A quest is a pursuit or a hunt for something. In fables a quest generally involved the search for a particular object or perhaps to slay a dragon.

When you embark on a 91 Day Quest, you are beginning a journey with a goal in mind and a time frame in which to achieve that goal.

When you have a very clear goal in mind and a deadline for achieving it, it simplifies your task.

A journey without a destination is simply wandering. A pursuit without an end goal or objective is meandering and pointless.

When you combine a pursuit with a time frame, a road map and an end goal, you bring together the ingredients to formulate a successful endeavor.

Figure out your goals (using this book as a guide), and you'll discover the purpose of your first Quest.

Why 91 Days?

Businesses work on a quarterly system, so it's logical to assume that a quarter - which is 13 weeks - would be an ideal time frame to use for a Quest.

You will often see 90 days as a time frame for a goal. I prefer 91 days because that is exactly 13 weeks, and it's easy to keep track of everything on a week to week basis.

What if I need more than 91 days?

If you need more than 91 days in order to complete your Quest, don't panic. I always suggest that instead of extending your quest by a week or two, you actually begin a new quest for another 13 weeks to achieve the goal.

I will talk more about this at the end of the book, but I advocate using the **P.E.A.R. System**:

Plan – Execute – Assess – Repeat

If you come to the end of your 91 Day Quest and you realize that you are not going to reach your longer-term goal, assess how your Quest went and then repeat the process with an adjusted 91 Day Quest.

In doing things this way, you will stay on track and you will progress, but you will not lose your momentum because you will come from a position of strength and change instead of a position of trying to catch up or running behind.

Don't stress - just start another quest.

"91 days will affect the next 20 years"

It takes 21 days to develop a new habit, so the saying goes. But you're not working on developing a new habit. Or even abolishing old ones.

You're changing your financial future. The future of your business.

I work with business owners (mostly ones in the health and wellness professions – chiropractors, fitness coaches, personal trainers, etc.) to do several things:

- Become THE person in their town to go to for their industry.

- Creating passive income (why? Because most of my clients are on the trading-hours-for-dollars hamster wheel when we start working together)

- Develop these income streams as the way to be EVERYWHERE in their town – so they are on a massive marketing kick.

- Use some of their new income streams to open doors for publicity – like radio spots, interviews, etc.

Why write this book?

I solve two big problems for my clients.

1. "I'd love to take time off, but I can't. If I'm not seeing clients, I'm not making money."

2. "I'd love to spread the word about my business and beat my local competition, but I already advertise and I don't know what else to do."

To be honest, I can't help everyone personally. I only work with one person per city (or ZIP Code, depending on how large a city is), per industry. Also, I mainly focus on health and wellness professionals. Third, some people can't afford my services. (That's why I wrote this book, and why I also offer group coaching, workshops, webinars and more – to help as many people as I can.)

That being said, I think EVERY business owner can use at least SOME of the strategies I teach, and I have a soft spot for business owners. I have a large local business group (Carolina Business Outreach Network), and I have a large online business group as well (Southern Home Business Moms).

I hear a lot about the day-to-day struggles that business owners face.

This book is my way of trying to help three groups of business owners:

- The ones who are struggling

- The ones who are doing well, but could be doing so much better. They aren't maximizing their income potential, and they don't have passive income to go along with their primary business model.

- The ones who are getting burnt out because they are on the trading-hours-for-dollars hamster wheel.

1 CHANGING YOUR WAY OF THINKING

You have to change your way of thinking.

I was once told by a client that I have a very unique way of looking at things.

I suppose this is true, but it is definitely a skill that anyone can learn because I was not always like this.

Let me explain.

When I hear a client or a colleague talking about his or her business, my mind instantly goes to thinking about all of the different income streams that they could be generating by simply re-purposing things that they are already doing.

You're going to hear me use the phrase re-purposing a lot, so let me go a little in depth about what I mean by that. Then I will explain the rest.

If you have a 2 L plastic soda bottle, once you are

done drinking the soda you clean it out, cut off the top, and use the bottom part as a planter. You have re-purposed that empty soda bottle.

In other words you took the basic product, made a few changes, and used it for an entirely different purpose. That purpose is every bit as useful as the original purpose.

You can do the same thing with your business.

Do you have a newsletter? If you have six different newsletters you can certainly take the best parts of each newsletter and use those to create a Hotsheet, a book or some other informational product. You have re-purposed the content.

Maybe you don't even have a newsletter yet. As an example, perhaps you are a chiropractor and you know a great deal about nutritional supplements. You can take that knowledge that you often use to answer common questions for patients about their health, and you could turn that into a monthly newsletter, a book, an e-book or any other type of informational product. You have taken the same information and use it for a different purpose.

Perhaps you have a popular blog, and one of the posts is a favorite of your readers. It gets a lot of hits from the search engines, and you get a lot of comments about it. You could take that blog post, edit it, and turn it into a report. You could even expand on it and turn it into an entire book. Again, you have re-purposed the content.

This is a long term plan. It's 91 Days at a time, which is 13 weeks. It's not an overnight solution.

Setting up additional income streams will take time. It takes time to create the income streams. It also takes time to generate revenue from those income streams. And it takes time to use those income streams for marketing and to generate some buzz/PR.

The good news is that once you have them in place and they are an integral part of your sales funnel (and once they have been marketed properly) they will become ongoing streams of income that will feed into your main business model.

2 WHY SHOULD YOU HAVE ADDITIONAL PAY STREAMS?

Stability - if you think about how a table works, the stability comes with having four legs. If you only have one or two, it will not help keep the table standing upright.

The same thing can be said with income streams and cash flow with your business. If you have a number of income streams that all flow into your main business model, it helps to provide a level of stability that will not happen if you only have one or possibly two income streams.

Let me give you an example.

I live in an area that is prone to hurricanes. If I have a retail store and my only source of income is when people come into my store and purchase from me, what happens if a hurricane hits? It doesn't even have to hit my area. If it comes close enough for everyone to evacuate as a precautionary measure, it still means that I have no foot traffic for at least several days. If a hurricane actually *hits* my area, it could mean that I have no foot traffic at all in my store for weeks or months. For most business owners this would mean closing their doors.

If I have other income streams (especially if those are online, which is what I mostly teach) then even if my income does decline because of circumstances beyond my control in my local area, I could still have enough profits generated through my other income streams to help weather the storm (no pun intended).

This falls under the wisdom of "Don't put all of your eggs in one basket." It's always a wise thing to have more than one income stream and more than one way to have income generated.

Lead generation - most business owners generate leads by purchasing advertising, or they can also have referrals, cold calls, direct mail, etc. There is nothing wrong with having these ways of reaching out to potential customers or clients. It can be a very effective strategy if it's done properly.

But having additional income streams can also mean you have additional sources of lead generation that not only bring leads into your main business (whether that is a retail store, your office, or whatever the case may be) it means that your lead generation sources can also be generating income as well.

If you have a number of informational products that refer back to your business - an example might be a book, report, etc., that a wedding planner might produce that gives 10 wedding disasters to avoid - then not only will you generate income from selling that particular product (or products), but the products themselves will refer back to your main business and can provide leads for your ultimate goal - to have someone higher you or come into your store and be your customer or client.

Authority - if you're in a highly competitive field, this is one of the main reasons why you want to have additional streams of income that also help boost your credibility and your authority.

Having a book, workshop or some other authoritative product will put you head and shoulders above your competition.

A good example for this would be chiropractors - which chiropractor are you going to choose: the one who just has an ad in the local phone book, or the one who was a published author and is an established authority in his or her field?

Yep, door number two. And a smart chiropractor would trumpet the fact that he or she is the author of this book on everything that he or she does - business cards, have copies of the book in the waiting room when the patients are sitting there, announce it in newsletters, etc.

Education - I am going to use the chiropractor example again, because I find the chiropractors have an amazing amount of information that they can share with the public - but there are many other professions that can do the same.

Many chiropractors are also on a crusade to help educate people about the benefits of nutrition, spinal health, and holistic health - they aren't just about adjusting your spine and then sending you home - so they make great candidates for this kind of marketing.

You can have products that help educate your current clients and customers or you can also have products that are focused on educating potential clients and customers.

Accountants, attorneys, OB/GYN's, cosmetologists, and a host of others - just about every professional has seen people make the same mistakes over and over will they hear the same questions over and over. Simply warn people of all these mistakes or answer the questions that are frequently asked and you already have an excellent income stream in the making.

Helping more people - let's face it: you can't help everybody. At least you can't *personally* help everybody. You only have so many hours in the day, and not everybody lives close enough to you.

By having informational products that take your expertise and knowledge and put them into formats that make them widely available to thousands or millions of people, you will instantly increase the number of people that you can help.

You may not be able to help every single person personally, but you certainly will be able to touch an enormous number of lives simply by putting your thoughts into products that can be accessed 24/7, 365 days a year.

You can literally change the world, simply by sharing your story with it.

Sales funnel - there are going to be people who are not ready to hire you right on the spot or make a purchase from you right away. By offering some low priced or free informational products that point back to your main business, you can help bring potential customers into your sales funnel and make it easier for them to know you, like you, trust you, and purchase from you.

Even if you offer free informational products, you can still make that a source of income, so don't think that the only way you can make money from an informational product is charging a dollar amount for it. (We'll talk about free vs. paid products later on.)

Higher profits per sale - for business owners there are a limited number of ways that you can increase your revenue. In general, you can increase the number of customers you have, increase the frequency that people purchase from you, or you can make a higher dollar amount per sale. By having an assortment of informational products that people can purchase in addition to your main offering, you can increase your dollar amount per sale, or you can have people purchase from you more often because you offer a number of different products.

More sources of revenue - this goes to diversification. It's a slightly different take on the "don't put all your eggs in one basket" motto.

If you have a number of sources of your revenue (a mixture of informational products and other products and services, online and off-line sources, etc.) it helps to contribute to your overall financial stability.

Let's take a look at Donald Trump. Love him or hate him, the man makes money. And the truth is that most people could not afford to hire him for even 10 minutes of his time to help pick his brain and learn what he knows about real estate and other moneymaking ideas.

But everybody can afford to pay 10 or 20 bucks to go to the bookstore and purchase a book and read 200 pages of what he thinks.

It's a source of income that helps secure his authority, diversify his income, educate more people, reach a larger audience, and adds to his bottom line.

You can do the same thing.

Higher profit margins - most physical goods have a profit margin of 50% or less. Digital Products can have profit margins of 90% or more. You can sell a product for a lot less money but still make a decent profit if you have Digital Products for sale.

More products is a good thing. More products with higher profit margins are even better.

Reaching a wider audience - this ties in somewhat with the education benefit that I mentioned earlier, along with helping more people. It just doesn't sound quite as altruistic as those do. The end result is the same, however. You can only knock on so many doors and meet so many people personally. By having informational products you can reach a huge audience That will filter down into your main business, and it can still make a nice profit for you.

Freedom - one of the bad things about providing a service or having a retail establishment is that you literally trade your hours for dollars most of the time. If you're in the service industry – OB/GYN, chiropractor, lawyer, accountant, or whatever - then you know the hamster wheel of trading hours for dollars very well. If you take any time off, you don't get paid.

Having multiple sources of income that are products which can be sold 24/7, 365 days a year allows you to have a freedom that you did not have before. Imagine going to bed and then waking up with more money than what you had before you went to sleep.

Imagine going on vacation and having more money in the bank a week later when you come home than you did when you left.

It may sound amazing (and it is) but it's not a fairytale. This is the kind of passive income generation that you can have if you have informational products that are generating income for you on autopilot.

It doesn't happen overnight, and it takes work to get everything set up. But the results are amazing.

Referrals - some of the people that purchase your informational products and learn more about you and your business are not going to become clients or customers of your main business.

However there will be a number of them that will realize that you are offering something that would be of great benefit to someone that they know.

This is why all of your informational products need to have a call to action where people can direct their friends and family to learn more about you.

A good example would be to have a book or other informational product that says towards the end something along the lines of "If you know of anyone who would enjoy learning more about what you just learned about, send them to my site so that they can get their free gift" - and then have an incentive for someone to join your mailing list and then they can get into your sales funnel just like the person who had just purchased one of your products did.

You can even have a special gift for those who find your site via a referral. (Have a spot for "Referred by" on your site.)

More clients - this really is everything that we have

talked about up until this point. You will have more clients wanting your products or services because they've already gotten to know you through your informational products.

Business for generations - leaving a legacy - one of the things about having a business is that certain businesses are difficult to leave/will to your children unless they decide to follow the same career path that you do.

Let's to go back to our Donald Trump example again. Yes, he has children that follow in his footsteps as far as real estate and other business ventures, but the books that he is produced and the other informational products that he has created will be a source of revenue for his children for decades after he is gone.

It's an amazing thing to think about. You can create a business (and a legacy) that can help provide an income for your children, your grandchildren, and beyond - even if they don't decide to do the same thing that you have done for a career.

Work once, get paid forever - this is the power that musicians and authors have known for years -

you work once and get paid for that work forever. Musicians and authors do that through royalties. You can do that through royalties and also a number of other options - the possibilities are unlimited.

Now, for two tools for the trade to help you:

Your two new best friends:

1. An auto-responder

2. Dragon NaturallySpeaking

No matter which options you choose for your informational products, these two tools are indispensable.

Let me explain what they both are and why they are so important.

An **auto-responder** is simply a tool that you can use in order to send out emails and electronic newsletters. You can also use it to help deliver home study courses, membership material and a host of other things.

The best part about an auto responder is that it can deliver the material that you want to have sent out in whatever time frame you want it to happen.

Let's say you want to have a welcome message for someone when they first sign up for your list. You would also like for them to be able to get a special report at the same time. Seven days after they sign up, you would like to have an email sent to them thanking them for joining your list again and also inviting them to download a chapter of your book for free. 30 days after they sign up you may have an email sent out that invites them to come to a workshop or a webinar.

The possibilities are endless, and an auto responder helps automate the process so that you are not manually sending out emails. Everything is automatic and it happens without you even paying attention to it.

There are a number of auto responders out there. You can choose anyone that you would like, but I personally recommend using GetResponse - it is the auto responder that I use and I am very pleased with how user-friendly it is and how many options there are available.

The second tool that you are going to want to invest in is Dragon NaturallySpeaking.

People ask me how in the world they are going to create all of these different informational products. They think it's going to take a long time and they're going to be hunched over a computer typing their little hearts out for weeks and months on end in order to make even one small informational product.

The truth is very different if you have the right tools.

This tool will help you turn your speech into text. Quite simply, all you have to do is speak as you naturally would into a headset and the software will have the words appear on the screen almost as quickly as you can speak them.

It is not unusual for me to be able to produce 2000 words in an hour easily - and I can do it even faster if I have everything outlined and ready to go ahead of time instead of having to pause and edit as I go along.

Yes, you can pay to have someone create your content for you. I have certainly helped clients do this before, and it is certainly a viable option.

But if you use a speech to text tool like Dragon NaturallySpeaking, you will have your own voice and personality infused in your informational products so that people will actually get to know how you really are, and they will be able to get a sense of who you are through the way that you speak and write.

Using this tool also makes sure that you keep your tone conversational and you should have everything more easily understood because it gives you the sense of speaking to a friend or a client - you are going to get all technical and you're going to try and make sure that you explain things in a very easy to understand manner because you are speaking it out loud.

I have purchased Dragon NaturallySpeaking through Amazon.com and I have also purchased a newer version at Best Buy. I'm sure you can probably find it in other places, but those are the places I have personally purchased them from.

Even if you have used a previous older version of Dragon NaturallySpeaking, I highly suggest that you get an updated version because the updated versions are miles ahead of what the older versions were like. The first version that I ever bought was a 10.0 or something close to it. The difference between that one and the 12.0 is absolutely amazing - and I was already a huge fan of it before.

Do yourself a favor and invest in this particular piece of software. You will make your money back from it simply from the time-saving aspect of it - you can use it to write emails, you can use it to write blog posts, create your informational products, and a host of other things. It will increase your productivity in all aspects of your business.

You'll need to go back and edit what you write, but I truly believe that the time saved in the original creation is well worth the investment in this software.

If you're thinking:

"This sounds like a lot of work. I don't have time for this. I have a business to run!"

- It is a lot of work, but it's worth it.
- If you **truly** don't have time for it, check out my **Resources** page after reading this book for done-for-you options.

3 INCOME STREAM OPTIONS

Please note: I have *never* had a client create every single one of these. Ever. At *most* they may create 8 or 10, and that's not common.

Every business is different – use these options to choose the *best* three for you, then see if you'd like to add 3 more. Don't feel pressured to try them all, or even a third of them all.

Options

I am going to briefly discuss pay stream possibilities for you. As you work through the exercises later in the book I will elaborate on some of my comments, but for right now I just want to give you a brief description of all the different pay streams that are available to you. I think that they will blow your mind.

If you count the different income stream options and you add in the different levels for each (free, paid and premium), **you have around 60 different options** for your income streams.

Newsletters

Most business owners will have some type of newsletter that they send out to a mailing list. If you do not have one, this will be the very first one that I suggest you begin with. Not only is it very simple to do, but it can be scheduled to be sent out automatically, and it can be a huge asset to your business.

You will need to have an auto responder in order to have an effective newsletter delivery system - as I've said before, I recommend GetResponse.

You have three options when it comes to offering a newsletter.

Free - this is a must for every business. Having a free newsletter that is sent out will not necessarily mean it will not generate income for you. There are a number of ways that you can make a free newsletter a very profitable pay stream for you.

Paid (low-cost) - there are a number of newsletters that charge a nominal fee each month for their subscribers. There is some added benefit, of course, to pay the monthly fee as opposed to simply receiving the free newsletter each month.

Depending on your business, you could offer information that provide some kind of value to your subscribers or you could simply offer some other special gift to your subscribers that makes the paid version of the newsletter a no-brainer.

Paid (Premium) - did you know that there are some newsletters that charge hundreds of dollars per month for the subscribers? It might seem unbelievable to you, but there are a number of industry-specific newsletters that provide such valuable information that the subscribers will happily pay large amounts of money in order to subscribe.

Almost any industry or business can offer this type of newsletter - it simply take some creative thinking in order to make it work.

Hotsheets

What's a Hotsheet? It's a report that goes by the formula "one problem, one solution, 20 pages or less."

Pick one issue your potential clients have, write a Hotsheet solving it, and you're done.

Hotsheets are somewhat more elaborate than most newsletters, but they still are fairly simple to create. You also have your free and your paid options, and generally speaking the criteria for your free and paid report are about the same as your free and paid newsletters.

Books

As far as I'm concerned, books are the holy Grail as far as pay streams go. There are so many benefits to being the author of your own book that it would take an entire book in and of itself in order to sing adequate praises for having your own book.

Books are also extremely versatile, and they can spin off so many other products.

In the category of books, you can have workbooks, journals, study guides, devotionals, or even textbooks. This one category can easily provide 10 different pay streams alone.

Books also add an incredible air of authority for the author. While your competitors will have a business card, you can actually hand a book that was written by you to your prospect.

Being a published author opens a number of doors for you. Press releases, book signings, interviews by the press – so many things are available for you that by being a published author, you can become a local celebrity, of sorts.

And, in turn, use that as leverage for your business to boom.

People also search for books on certain topics so that they can get answers to questions and solve problems. If you have a book that helps them with a particular issue, then it will certainly help you gain more clients or customers because readers of the book will want to know more about you and will want to do business with you. They've already read about your expertise.

Of course, in your book you want to promote your

newsletter, workshops, and any other pay streams that you have. This is over and above your main business, so you are having one pay stream help to promote all of your other ones.

I often have clients that ask if the printed book market is obsolete. My answer to that is a resounding no. While you also want to have electronic versions of your books, there are many people who prefer a physical book and also lend more credibility to you if you have a physical book in conjunction with an electronic version.

E-books

Having digital versions of your books is a good complement to your physical versions. I would not necessarily advise someone to *only* have a digital version of a book, but sometimes it is faster to get a digital version up and running and ready for sale than it is to have a physical version.

There are a number of different ways that you can offer an e-book for sale. Kindle is one popular option, or you can use a digital product sales and delivery option, such as E-junkie.

Workshops

Workshops are a fantastic way to get your name out in the community. When I talk about workshops I am talking about the in-person, hands-on workshops where you actually have a meeting room, an audience and you are physically present with everyone.

While there might be a few drawbacks to meeting in person instead of having a webinar, workshops can be an amazing tool in your pay stream arsenal.

Free - free workshops can be great if you do it on a limited basis. I don't normally suggest having a huge amount of free workshops. (Webinars are another story entirely - and we'll talk about those in a moment.) The reason why I suggest you have a limited number of free workshops is because it does take a great deal of time and effort to set up, and it can be very time-consuming to the point of taking away your precious time from other income generating activities.

One good thing about free workshops is that they can be recorded and then packaged for distribution on your website. (If you would like to have them available for free or paid for those who cannot attend in person, that is up to you.)

Paid - having a paid workshop is an excellent way to not only generate immediate revenue from having the workshop, but it also helps to get the word out about your business and about your other pay streams.

If you have a paid in-person workshop, you can always package it by having it recorded and then having the workshop materials available online as well and then sell it. This way you have the paid workshops that you do in person that can generate income, but you have an additional pay stream from the sale of the recorded workshops that will be an automated pay stream. (This is also an example of re-purposing content to a degree.)

Webinars

I love webinars. Webinars are one of the greatest

tools that you can use to help build your business. As long as you have your computer or some other device that will let you conduct a webinar wherever you are, you can work your business in any location.

As far as I'm concerned, you have all the benefits of a workshop without the hassle of trying to find a physical location for the workshop, the prep time to help make sure you have everything set up in the physical location or workshop, and the time needed to help plan the workshop.

While you certainly need planning in order to have an effective webinar, the logistics of finding the location like you would with a workshop are not a factor.

Finding a quiet place to hold webinar might be a challenge, however, if you have kids in the house. (Just an FYI from experience.) Although (as is my case) I have that as part of my "personality" - people know I often work from home and have 3 kiddos, so my attendees at my webinars know I may have some background noise. (Not a lot, but some.) If that bothers people, they aren't really my target audience. Most of my audience is made up of parents, so they understand the interruptions, and some even say they find it encouraging that I work around the sporadic interruptions.

You can have free and paid options for your webinars just as you can for your workshops. They can be recorded and then packaged so that they can be available on your website, and you can even have webinar versions of in person workshops that you might have.

Webinars are an excellent way to expand your customer base to a national or worldwide market. Having in-person workshops severely limit the scope and scale of your reach. Having webinars frees you from those constrictions.

CD

A CD can be one of the simplest ways to get started, especially if you have enough material to give a speech that will last anywhere from 20 minutes up to an hour.

Jot down your notes, rehearse what you're going to say, and then begin recording. It's very simple and it doesn't take a whole lot of work to do. There are plenty of fulfillment companies that can take your audio file and convert it into a CD, or you could even burn CDs on your own if you would like.

As with all the other options you can choose to have your CD as a free giveaway or you can choose to have it for sale on your site. You could even use it as a type of deluxe audio business card. It can be an amazing marketing tool!

DVD

Another option is to record one of your workshops, webinars, or seminars and turn it into a DVD. Plenty of fulfillment companies will do this for you, or you can do it yourself - my suggestion would be that for a DVD to be professional, you would like to have someone edit it. If that is not your forte, I would suggest hiring someone to do it for you.

Using it for a free giveaway is an option, along with having it as a paid option or even a premium option (depending on the material on the DVD).

Conference calls

You can have a conference call that is free or paid, just like with all of the other options.

I like conference calls because you can have them anywhere in the world - all you need is a cell phone. It's also very easy for people to dial-in because they don't have to be in front of a computer like to do on a webinar - making it very convenient for people to participate.

You can have one every week, or you can have one monthly - whichever one you ready to commit to on a regular basis is what you should use.

There are a number of conference call options, but one that I use is freeconferencecall.com. The basic service is wonderful, but they also have paid options so that you can upgrade if you would like.

Having recorded conference calls can be a tremendous tool on your website as well - it lets visitors to your site learn about you and get to know you better.

You can choose to have a conference call that is centered around your particular business, or you can have it geared towards a more general audience.

For example, if you are a business coach your conference call can center around certain aspects of business success or you can have it as a more general motivational type conference call. It really depends on what the end goal for your calls is.

Retreats

Retreats are an excellent way to provide a unique experience for your clients/customers. They can be for a weekend, a week, or even longer.

Choosing a scenic location (beach house, mountain cabin) adds to the value and desirability of the retreat.

This can be a high-dollar item in your income stream arsenal.

"Boot camps"

Do you have a business that would provide great material for a six or 12 week boot camp?

Maybe your business deals with some type of transformation - whether it's a change in eating habits, or personal health, or perhaps some type of habit you want to change - having a 6 to 12 week boot camp of sorts can be a great kickoff to a longer program, or it can simply be a program in and of itself.

You don't necessarily have to choose a time that's within 6 to 12 weeks, but that seems to be a very common time frame to use, and allows enough time for people to really make huge changes in their lives. It's the perfect time frame to help people create new habits and abolish older habits.

You can set up these boot camps either as a membership site, or you can have them delivered via email with your auto-responder.

You don't have to be limited to one type of boot camp, either. You can have a number of boot camps going on at one time, especially if everything is automated. That's the beauty of having everything delivered automatically - it frees you up so that you are able to do other things, and you have pay streams that are delivered automatically to you, while they provide material automatically to the subscribers.

You can have payments for boot camps set up as either a one time payment, monthly payment, or even a weekly payment.

What sounds more affordable? Do you think a customer would buy a 12 week boot camp subscription for $50? Or do you think that they would be more likely to buy a 12 week boot camp subscription for only seven dollars a week?

Surprisingly, even though it would be cheaper to pay the one time payment of $50 a lot of people will go for seven dollars a week.

You can do a test on your market to see what kind of payment works better for you and for your customers - and you can always offer both: they can pay the payment upfront, or they can choose a higher amount but having small weekly payments instead. You may be surprised at what would work best for you and your customers or clients.

In-person conferences

Not for the faint of heart, this is a definite option if you can put the planning and the time into it. It can be a huge credibility boost, but I would suggest you having a lot more of the simpler pay streams in effect before you take this one on.

That being said, once you have enough of the following and in person conference can be an incredible pay stream, and it can be incredibly rewarding as well.

Unless your specialty is event planning, I would suggest you have help planning and in person conference.

Associations

This does not have to be as complicated as you

might think. You can easily start a local association in your area. You can either have an industry specific one for your particular business, or you can have a general business one if your ideal clients consist of business owners.

This is obviously not an information product, per se, but you can certainly have information products, out of the material that is presented at any association meetings (assuming, of course, that the material presented as yours).

E-courses

This has some similarities to the boot camp that was discussed earlier, but in e-courses can be much longer (or shorter) than a regular boot camp is. (I have seen some e- courses that are a year long, and some that are only 3 days.)

If you have a lot of material that can be converted into a series of daily or weekly lessons or action steps, you may want to consider creating an E-course.

You can have the lessons or action steps delivered

via the auto responder, or you can have a password-protected membership site in order to deliver the lessons.

"X of the month" options

One of the benefits that I stress when it comes to creating additional pay streams is that you are looking for recurring income - especially if the income is passive.

I know that you've all seen the fruit of the month club that people sometimes give as gifts. You basically pay a yearly or monthly fee and you can give a gift every month to someone.

Each month you receive a box of fruit - it's the gourmet kind, not the cheap stuff that you find a local store - and so instead of receiving one gift, you basically receive 12 gifts that are delivered throughout the year.

I've seen variations of this in all aspects of businesses - chocolate, fruit, lingerie, and a host of other things.

Sit down with a pen and paper and start jotting down some ideas as to what you could offer with your business has a _____ of the month club-type product or service.

It doesn't necessarily have to be a physical product in order to be offered this way.

One thing that I have suggested with one of my associates that has a candle business is that he offer a "Scent of the Month" Club. Each subscriber pays a few dollars a month, and they get a new scent sample each month. PLUS each subscriber gets a coupon that is good for either a free candle with a monthly purchase, or they get X dollars off with a monthly purchase.

In charging for being a member of the scent of the month club, not only does my client get to send out samples to people without it costing anything for him upfront, the customers get to sample the new scents and also get a coupon that is worth more than what they're actually paying for their membership.

They never know exactly what they're going to get

for their coupon each month, so there's also that element of surprise - but they are *never* disappointed.

Use your imagination to develop ways to grow your customer base without it costing you anything out of pocket upfront.

Memberships

Having memberships as a pay stream is an incredibly flexible model to use. You can have the same levels that you would with many of the other pay streams - free, paid with a low monthly charge and high volume or a premium membership that runs on a high dollar amount with lower volume - but you also have many different versions and platforms that you can use for your members.

You can have a membership forum, or you can have a membership that delivers material via email, or you can have conference calls, webinars, etc.

You are only limited by your imagination when it comes to the format your membership can take.

Having a membership model provides a large number of benefits, and not just because it's a pay stream. It also helps to promote you as an authority in your field, it helps you to develop a following - much like Seth Godin talks about in his book *Tribes* - and it also develops a loyal group of customers that look forward to your communications each day/week/month, so you are free to promote your other pay streams to a very receptive audience.

Another attractive feature to having a membership model is that you can develop a very strong recurring income from it. You can charge a monthly fee in order for someone to be able to be a member in your forum/email list/etc. One of the benefits of having a lower monthly fee is that you will have less of the problem of attrition - losing members - and you should be able to sell your memberships more quickly. (That's not a guarantee, though.)

On the other hand, if you have a higher-priced membership where you charge a premium in order for someone to be a member and you provide excellence material and benefits to someone who is a part of that elite group, you can develop a substantial income while also cultivating a very loyal following.

The membership model is a great way for you to also get referrals for your main business from the group of subscribers.

Memberships are also a great way to let potential clients and customers get to know you a little more intimately than they would just from your public blog or website. This is actually one of the main attractions for many memberships - the chance to connect a little bit more closely to someone whose work or business they admire.

Having exclusive material is another benefit. If you have a book or workshop, for example, and you offer a membership that will give even more detailed information than they would find simply in the book or workshop, this can be a huge draw.

You can even have a membership that focuses on a particular niche that is within your overall field. I'll use myself for this example: with my book I talk about business owners and particular types of service providers. One of my favorite groups to work with happens to be chiropractors. I could offer a membership that is exclusively for chiropractors to help them develop their additional pay streams and automate them. The material would be very specific, and it would be geared exclusively to the wants and needs and issues that would apply to chiropractors.

You can use this example and change it to whatever your particular business may have apply. It's entirely possible to set up 10 or 15 different memberships that stem from one particular workshop or book.

Exploring the scope of how memberships can play into your overall pay stream strategy would take a whole book in and of itself. I hope that the examples that I just gave, however, will help get you thinking about some of the possibilities.

Merchandise

This isn't a pay stream that most people think about, but there are ways for you to use merchandise in order to help promote your other pay streams. Not only can you sell the merchandise to help foster a sense of community, but you can use merchandise such as T-shirts, coffee mugs, etc. in order to use them as giveaways or other "freemiums."

This is especially useful if you already have a following. Come up with a logo and some slogans, design some shirts and mugs, and have some fun! You can either work with a local person in order to create your merchandise, or you can use a platform such as Café press or Zazzle.

This isn't something that you should discount offhand. I recently saw a huge display of branded merchandise for cereal companies – T-shirts, insulated cups, coffee mugs, plates and bowls - that were proudly plastered over with the logos of the companies involved.

Think about this - not only are people paying for the merchandise, but everything that they use or wear is an advertisement for that company. Talk about a great way to make money while getting more customers! You can certainly do the same thing with your own brand, your own website, and your own company. The sky's the limit!

Skype groups

Skype groups are actually a combination of different pay streams, but it's such a unique and new concept that I wanted to mention it as its own pay stream to get your mind around the idea.

Most people are familiar with Skype - it lets you talk with people all over the world for free. You can also use video, or you can simply use voice.

One of the neat things about Skype is that you can actually create groups with Skype.

There is a tutorial on how to do this with Skype, so I'm not going to reinvent the wheel until you how to do it. The important thing to realize is that you can make groups on Skype and that you can generate income from this.

You can set up a Skype that is a mastermind group, or a networking group, or simply a discussion group. You can have it be an exclusive group of individuals that meet every week or every month in order to have a discussion. In between the voice discussions you can have chat rooms with Skype so people can carry on a conversation in between the voice communications.

You can think of it as a conference call that also has chatting in between.

People can pay every month or every year in order to subscribe. You can also have a limited duration group - like one that meets each week for 91 days (13 weeks).

Lots of things you can do with this unique tool, and most people are familiar with Skype because the use it all ready to communicate with loved ones who are long-distance.

Mastermind groups

Mastermind groups can take many different forms. You can have some that are in person and you meet locally. You can also have a Skype group or a conference call.

The important thing about mastermind groups is that you meet on a fairly frequent basis, and you set up a regular time to communicate with everyone. There's also a sense of accountability, and you need to make sure that everything that is said within the group, *stays* within the group.

Some mastermind groups are free, but there are some that charge a membership fee in order to belong to it.

In general, mastermind groups are fairly small. Most of the ones that I have seen have fewer than 10 members. (Of course, you can form more than one mastermind group.)

Special cases

Assess your assets - every business has unique assets that is available only to that particular business. There's no way that I can cover everything that might fall under this category, but I can give you a particular example.

I have a client who - in addition to her primary business - also has a talk show, and all of those shows have been recorded. In talking to her and trying to uncover what types of assets she has in her business, I suggested that as an additional pay stream she could offer to take those transcripts and create books for the business owners out of those and charge for the service.

That is a unique case, obviously, but it shows you the type of thinking that you can develop so that you can look at your own business and create additional pay streams in many creative ways.

Paid vs. Free

Start free, then offer an "exclusive," "insider," "deluxe" version.

You can have an additional pay stream that does not have to have a purchase price.

Let me explain.

The easiest example to use is a newsletter because that is something that is very common and most people are familiar with.

You can offer a free newsletter that is of no charge to the prospect. All they have to do is give their name and or email address and your newsletters show up in their inbox.

You can generate income from this a number of different ways.

A common way to do this is to offer your products and services via your newsletter so that people can purchase them at their leisure (these would be your informational products, or if you have products that you retail as your regular business you can include those as well if they are available from your website).

As a clarification - if you only use your newsletter to tell people to come into your store and purchase products or to contact you so that they can hire you for your services, that is not exactly an income stream from your newsletter. You are simply using your newsletter to help attract people to your main business.

In my personal opinion, in order for a newsletter to be considered an additional pay stream, it needs to be something that can have a certain degree of automation.

Gift certificates would be an ideal way to turn a newsletter into an additional income stream. You can also offer your informational products and you can make recommendations for other products that will give you an affiliate commission. (This will all become clearer later, so don't panic. I'm just trying to give you an overview right now.)

Another avenue that some people choose is to have a newsletter that is actually a product in and of itself. You would sell subscriptions to your newsletter the same way that someone would sell a subscription to an online magazine.

If you can provide exclusive information, tips, or other valuable information via your newsletter that people can't get other places, this might be a good place for you to start with an income stream.

If you decide to have a paid newsletter, you can choose to have a low-cost/high-volume newsletter or you can choose to have a high cost/lower volume newsletter. There are pros and cons to each business model to choose, and we will discuss more options when we discuss newsletters.

You can apply the above scenario to a number of

different things: reports, e-books, e- courses, webinars, etc.

Keep this in mind when we start talking about newsletters and other pay streams.

L. Shay Rockhold

4 OVERWHELMED?

There are a lot of options for you, and I know it can be bewildering.

So if you are just starting, I suggest focusing on what I call **The Savvy Six.**

These are 6 basic income stream categories that most businesses can do, and they are generally simpler to implement.

Best of all – if you only do these 6 categories, it's plenty. Combine the 6 categories with three options (Free – Paid – Premium) and you've got a potential 18 income streams (or more) from these categories alone.

So take a deep breath, grab a cup of coffee, and relax while I talk a little bit about the **Savvy Six.**

L. Shay Rockhold

5 THE SAVVY SIX

- Newsletters
- Books
- Workshops
- Webinars
- Hotsheets
- Memberships

You could base all of your income streams on these 6 categories alone.

You have three options for each income stream:

Free – Paid – Premium.

Plus you could have multiple books, multiple topics for workshops and webinars, and more.

That's a minimum of 18 income streams from these group of possibilities alone.

Best of all, I can almost guarantee that you're competition isn't doing all of these. *Offer what they aren't offering.*

L. Shay Rockhold

6 HOW TO APPROACH PRODUCT CREATION

Now that we've talked about different models for your income streams, we're going to talk about how to start creating those income streams.

There are two different approaches that I use. Neither one is better than the other. The approach you use depends strictly on what your comfort level is, and either one can be successful.

If you really don't have a preference as to which one you use, when I am done explaining them I will give you my suggestion for which one you choose when neither one is really your hot button.

Start small

Some of the clients that I work with really don't have the big picture in mind. They may not have a good idea of what they want their long-term pay stream picture to look like, so they might be intimidated by the process.

For these clients I suggest that they start small and

then expand what their beginning product is.

This is also a good way to start if you have one incredibly deeply ingrained core belief that you want to get across as part of your pay stream strategy.

Let me give you a few examples and show you how it can work.

Let's say you really aren't sure what you want to do as part of the big picture. You really can't imagine having 10 or 12 pay streams in six months, but you do want to start somewhere.

You can start with a newsletter, pack it full of tips and suggestions, answer questions, etc.

Once you have six of those, you should have enough for a report. Once you have 15 or 20, you should have enough for a book.

Or you can start with something very simple like a 2000 word report that tackles some question/problem that most of your clients have. Maybe you're a divorce attorney and you know of one big issue that people that are getting married should know about. Maybe it's all about prenuptial agreements, or maybe it's all about talking to your future spouse about what would happen if something went wrong.

Perhaps you're a chiropractor and you constantly see the effects of poor nutrition with your clients. The message that you want to get out to the world is how you can improve your nutrition and improve your overall health. So you can start with a newsletter or a report that explains what people can do to help improve their overall health by improving their nutrition.

Once you start getting your feedback from these types of reports or newsletters, you may find that you have a very specific direction that you see your informational products going towards.

It's a gradual process, but it can be a very effective one because you are taking feedback from a smaller product and using it to add to what you already have and develop it into something that is much larger and complex.

Start big

Then I have clients who are the exact opposite. I have literally sat down with clients who have a 50,000 word manuscript already for a book that they have been wanting to do for years because they have a specific message that they want to shout out to the world. They simply did not know where to go to start.

For these clients, having them start small is silly. They already have their major product - although it might need some editing or reworking in order to fit into their overall pay stream plan, it truly is (for the most part) done.

Some clients don't necessarily have a manuscript done, but they have ideas immediately about what they would like to do for a book or workshop or a seminar. They can't get the ideas out quickly enough - they already know what the big picture is going to be as far as their pay stream plan, but they don't really have all the smaller pieces in place yet.

So for these clients all they need to do is create,

polish and perfect their large product and then take sections of that in order to create a workshop or a report or a newsletter.

What will you choose?

Chances are when you read those two descriptions, one of those resonated with you.

But if neither one of those really rang your bell, my suggestion would be to start very small - with a newsletter or perhaps a short report - and then expand from there.

You can do this with the goal of having at least six pay streams in six months. The process will be fairly painless and simple. Once you began your first pay stream, you will find that the process of starting new pay streams will become simpler and simpler as time goes on.

There's a reason for this - you are actually going to start changing the way that you look at your business and look at yourself.

And my job is to help you.

Plan – Create – Polish - Publish - Promote

This is going to be your 5-step process for everything you create.

Even if you have someone help you with the polishing and promoting aspects of it, you can still use this system for whenever you have someone else involved in the process.

The first part is planning.

The way I do this is to create a very simple outline of whatever product I am creating. You can do this as a very simple bullet list, or you can simply have a format of 10 frequently asked questions that you see all the time.

Whatever you choose for your topic (or topics), simply make a list of those topics that you want to cover in your product.

The reason why I love Dragon NaturallySpeaking so much is because the way I work is I will make an outline of the points that I want to cover, do any research or jot down any notes that I need to in order to do my writing, and then I will take a block of time to sit down with Dragon NaturallySpeaking and speak my thoughts into words.

I am not going to lie. It's awkward at first to sit in front of your computer and talk to nobody.

But after a while you get used to it, and you kind of train yourself to work this way.

Back to the subject - once you have your outline and you know which points you want to cover, you then go back and elaborate on your points. If you are working on a larger work - such as a book or maybe a workshop - pace yourself. Your planning process is going to take a little bit longer because you have more material that you need to outline, and you also need to organize your material in such a way so that it flows easily.

Once you have everything written - your outline is done, all of your points of been made, everything has been fleshed out - then comes the part where you polish your product.

You are going to check over it, edit it, send it to people to review for you and give you ideas on how to make it better, etc. This is a perfect time to get some feedback and learn how effective your product is and also if there is anything that you have missed.

If there are questions about some of the material you have covered, you have the option of either going back in editing your existing product so that you can include the additional material. The other option is that you actually can create a brand-new product around the additional material. The option that you choose is going to depend on the product that you are creating, the audience that you are trying to reach, and how well the material flows with your existing material.

A good example would be for this particular book. I have many people who ask about marketing (and we will cover some of that in a moment), but I don't go in depth with marketing in this particular book and in my workshops because of a number of reasons:

There are a number of books, websites, consultants, etc., whose primary focus is helping people market their products - why should I reinvent the wheel? (Especially when I often speak to marketing people in order to get ideas for helping to market my own stuff.)

Marketing - especially with online marketing and social media - is constantly changing. The steps that I teach for creating products are pretty standard, and they won't change too much in the years to come. There may be additional tools, or there might be some additional options, but for the most part the basic principles are the same. Again, I feel that this is a better use of my time to play to my strengths and to give you the best possible experience in teaching you my area of expertise.

Now that you have created your plan for your product, and you have polished your product, now comes the part where you promote your product.

I am going to talk some about your personal promotion later on in this book, but I will also be sharing some different ideas that you can use for promotion. This does not mean that I'm going to give you a step-by-step marketing plan, but I will give you a basic outline of what you can do to help promote your additional pay streams in addition to any other marketing and advertising that you may already be doing or looking into doing.

For every product that you create, this is going to be your basic process. Once you plan, polish, and promote - you simply rinse and repeat, over and over.

As you add your pay streams to your repertoire of products and services, you will refer to your other products and services in each product and service that you offer.

So part of your promotion is going to be through your other pay streams. So for example, if you are conducting a workshop then you will also be promoting your books, newsletter, webinars, etc., in that workshop.

If you have a newsletter, you are going to be promoting your webinars, workshops, books, etc., in your newsletter.

If you have a free newsletter, and you also offer a paid version of it, you will promote the paid version in the free version.

Choose three for this 91 Day Quest

You can expand once you have the first three income streams in place, but for your initial Quest you should only have three income streams at most.

YOUR 91 DAY QUEST

You're going to work on your three income streams simultaneously.

Week 1 – Plan

You will have four action steps to complete for this week:

1. Check out what your competition is doing.
2. Analyze your current business model.
3. Choose your three income streams that you are going to develop.
4. Outline what your key points are going to be for your three income streams.

What is your competition doing? That can help guide your additional pay streams.

Are your competitors published authors? Probably not. That would be one HUGE advantage for you.

Do they conduct workshops? Webinars? Do they have generic newsletters, or are their newsletters customized and packed with info?

How about YOUR newsletters? Do you have some generic newsletter service that sends out industry-specific (but bland and impersonal) newsletters to anyone on your list? Do you have control of your list?

My suggestion for your three income streams would be to have a newsletter and a book, then add another complementary pay stream. The third pay stream is going to depend on what type of business you have and what your competition is doing, but you can take excerpts from your book or your newsletters and create either a short report or even a workshop/webinar.

Do not take less than a week to plan your income streams. You are going to make notes and then you're going to "sleep on them." The next day you are going to repeat the process.

The reason for this is to let your subconscious mind work while you sleep in order to help clarify what your path should be. This isn't some New Age mumbo-jumbo - it is simply the way that your mind works. When you think about something right before you go to sleep, your mind works on the issue while you sleep.

If you take a full week for this process, you give ample time for your mind to work and give you the right direction to go in.

Week 2 – 5 - Create

Now you are going work on your content. Take your outlines and start fleshing out your details.

Don't worry about editing at this point. Later on in your quest you are going to have two weeks for polishing and refining your content. Right now you simply want to get your notes down on paper (or in pixels) so that you can keep your pace steady and let your thoughts flow.

If you get too caught up in trying to edit as you write, you can lose your momentum and lose your train of thought.

Don't be impatient. You're not going to create something overnight. Take a little bit of time each day - an hour or two - and work on your content.

If you need to break up your work into five or six sessions of only 20 or 30 minutes each, feel free to do that.

Week 6 & 7 - Polish

Now you're going to start your editing. This is where you're going to take two weeks and polish/edit your work.

Don't rush this process. Take the entire two weeks to do your polishing. You are going to edit, then you are going to sleep on it. Then you can look at it with a fresh perspective the next day.

Do this over the course of the entire two weeks so that you are not rushing the process and you will have an end result that you will be happy with.

Week 8 & 9 – Publish

Now we are getting to the home stretch of your Quest.

You are going to be signing up for your auto responder and loading all of your newsletters and email messages into there, if newsletters are your choice.

You are also going to be finalizing your manuscript so that you can publish that, if a book is your choice.

Whatever you've chosen – books, newsletters,

workshops, etc. - now is the time to make them go live.

By this point you should have all of your polishing done and your products should be sparkling!

Now it's time to tell the world about what you have.

Week 10-13 – Promote

Now you have everything in place. You have your newsletter completed, your book published, etc.

Whatever your three income streams might be - now it's time to tell the world about what you have.

Once you have your three income streams up and running, choose your next three (if you want), or move on to another 91 Day Quest. (See the resources at the end of the book for ideas.)

Plan – Execute – Assess – Repeat

If you completed your quest on time, then it's time to choose which Quest you would like to do next.

If you would like to develop three additional income streams, then you can do that. If you would choose to focus on another aspect of your business - such as networking or becoming a business leader - then choose which ever one appeals to you. Maybe you'd like to encourage your team to pursue a group Quest.

If you fall short of your goal and you do not complete your quest in the 91 days, as part of your next 91 Day Quest you will assess how things went and then choose what your next 91 days will look like.

As an example, let's say that you did not complete all three of your income streams with your initial 91 Day Quest. You did complete two of them but you did not complete the third.

Your next 91 Day Quest could include completion of the third income stream that was not finalized in your initial quest, plus adding another to pay streams for your next 91 days.

To keep your timelines and your terminology consistent, the planning stage of your 91 Day quest in week number one will include an assessment of your previous 91 Day Quest, along with planning your next 91 Day Quest.

Think of it not as a linear process but more like a cycle.

7 EXAMPLES

I'm going to use a variety of examples to walk you through the process, using a cross-section of businesses.

John - an accountant

John's three income streams:

1. Newsletter
2. Book
3. Workshop

He has chosen these three because he already has a great deal of experience with information that he can easily put into a book. He is going to take excerpts of the book for his workshops and his newsletter.

He chooses the title "10 Dangerous Mistakes You Need to Avoid with Your Taxes." His workshop carries the same title, but it simply has an abbreviated version of the content of his book.

For his newsletter he chooses to give some basic information about what kinds of accounting mistakes you need to avoid for your business.

His newsletter is free, but he monetizes it by promoting his book and also promoting his workshops.

His workshops are free, but he monetizes them by promoting his book and it provides a nice stream of clients and referrals for him.

Liselle – a rep for a cosmetics company

Liselle's three income streams:

1. Book
2. Goodie Bag of the Month
3. Workshops

Liselle works from home as a rep for a cosmetics company. She is an independent contractor with a home-based business.

Because of the nature of her business, she has some restrictions as to what she can do and can't do. One of the restrictions is that she cannot use the company name in any of her income streams that she independently produces.

She has a newsletter that she already sends out every month, so she is chosen three different income streams for her Quest.

She decides to tell her personal story in her book: "Why I Choose to Work from Home." Because of the restrictions placed on her by her parent company, she does not mention her business by name. She simply states that she is a representative for a cosmetics company, and all of her contact information - email address, website, etc. - are all her personal sites and emails, not the ones provided through the company.

Because she is going to share her personal reasons for working at home, she knows that her story will resonate with a certain segment of the population. She's not seeking to brand herself as an expert in cosmetics. Instead she is looking to become an authority on working from home and she is seeking to promote herself as someone to come to if you are looking to start working from home.

She conducts two different types of workshops - one is product based and focuses on helping brides create the perfect look for their wedding makeup, and one is an introductory workshop for women who are thinking about starting to work from home. The workshop for wedding makeup is one that she charges for. The work at home workshop is free, and she monetizes it by promoting her book and also using this as a way to get customers, referrals and recruits.

She also desires to create a steady monthly income that isn't dependent on factors such as holidays or the seasons - she might get a surge in business around the holidays in the winter, but she might have a decline in the summer when many people are on vacation.

Because of this, she decides to create a Goodie Bag of the Month Club. She charges a certain amount every month, and her customers get a coupon that is worth twice the monthly charge. As an added bonus they also get an assortment of samples. (She checked with her company to make sure that she offered this in accordance with the terms and conditions of her company.)

Not only does she get a steady monthly income because of the subscriptions, but she gets business from the coupons that she sends out and also the samples.

She promotes her book at her workshops, and also in her newsletter and her Goodie bags.

Michelle – Realtor

Michelle's three income streams:

1. Newsletter
2. Workshops
3. Book

Michelle chooses to write a book about eight ways you can increase the curb appeal of your home and sell it faster. She conducts workshops with the same focus.

The workshops are free and she monetizes them by promoting her book. She finds the workshops to be a great way to get new clients and referrals.

Her newsletter is also free - she monetizes that by promoting her book. She also promotes her workshops in the newsletter as well.

Richard – Business Consultant/Coach

Richard's three income streams:

1. Book
2. CD
3. Retreat

Richard already has a newsletter that goes out every week and a number of workshops that he conducts, so for his Quest he wanted to expand on that.

Using a conglomeration of material from his workshops and from his newsletter, he designed the basic outline of his book from that and then added more material to update it and make it fresh.

He took one of his workshops and created a CD from it - taking a few of the key points and recording them. The CD is not very long - only about 15 minutes - but it does give a great overview of what his workshops are all about.

He chose to develop a weekend retreat as one of his income streams because he felt like it would be a great step for his current clients. He promotes his retreats at his workshops and through his newsletter, but a requirement of going to one of his retreats is that you must have attended at least one workshop prior to your registration for his retreat. He charges a high fee for his retreats. This is a reflection not only of the material that is covered but the exclusivity that is involved.

He promotes his workshops, book, and retreat through his CD and newsletter. His workshops are both free and paid, depending on the level. He has an introductory workshop that is free, and he has a more advanced workshop that is paid.

Patrick – Chiropractor

Patrick's three income streams:

1. Newsletter
2. Books
3. Workshops

Patrick's been a chiropractor for over 10 years, so he's got a lot of knowledge to share.

Plus his business is already impressive. He's got steady clients, and he has a thriving practice. Business is good! But he wanted it to be better.

He had a newsletter going out, but it was a template one, generically written for chiropractors. (He subscribed to a service that provided this.) He changed that to one written specifically for him and his practice.

Patrick easily has enough knowledge to write 10 books on various subjects, so he decided to work on one each Quest.

Using the material from the books, he created workshops. Then he, of course, used his newsletter to promote the books and workshops.

The books are bought by current patients, plus they can be used for prospecting, press releases, getting speaking engagements, etc.

91 Day Quest: for a Booming Business

8 CONCLUSION

Designing your ideal business takes time. Having a booming, balanced business is a way of maximizing your income without burning yourself out on the trading-hours-for-dollars hamster wheel.

Choose your Quest, work through it, and then begin a new one. After 6 months, a year, or more, you'll look at your business (and your lifestyle) and smile.

If you need help, be sure to visit www.91DayQuest.com.

RESOURCES

You have several options for your Quest.

Do it yourself

Plenty of options for help on my site: books, workshops, webinars, and (soon) a home-study course.

Extra guidance

If you'd like a little more help, I offer group coaching, and that is done online via emails, conference calls, and webinars.

Done-for-you option

Do you have too little time? Don't want to deal with the learning curve? Would you rather hand things over to someone else to create and take care of?

Contact me via my Contact Me page on my site for more information.

Visit my site for resources:

www.91DayQuest.com

91 Day Quest: for a Booming Business

TELL ME ABOUT YOUR QUEST

I'd love to hear about your Quest!

Use the Contact Me form at

www.91DayQuest.com

to let me know all about it!

ABOUT THE AUTHOR

Shay Rockhold is a business consultant in Charleston, SC.

She's the leader of the Carolina Business Outreach Network.

In addition, she's also a writer, mom of 3, Quest Coach, coffee lover, sci-fi fan and a public speaker.

She's available to speak to groups. Contact her via her site for availability and rates.

www.91DayQuest.com

www.ingramcontent.com/pod-product-compliance
Lightning Source LLC
Chambersburg PA
CBHW051730170526
45167CB00002B/869